"What You Need to Know"

Becoming an Amazon Delivery Service Partner (DSP)

Last Mile Delivery

Content of Information Book

PREFACE

I began writing this short information book on the Last Mile Delivery industry and Becoming an Amazon Delivery Service Partner because I have received hundreds of calls and emails for individuals wanting information about this opportunity. I hope this information in this book assist you on your journey in the New World of Last Mile Logistics.

It's fair to say that you could find some of this information on website, but I wrote this short information book to help the young logistics entrepreneur to understand the Last Mile Logistics Industry.

Imagine you've found yourself running out of kibble for your pet, and there's no way you can visit a store with a foreseeably long day scheduled at work. Thankfully, your favorite pet store has started offering one-day deliveries in your zip code. Smiling, you quickly hit some buttons on your mobile to order your pet's favorite food and some toys, too.

As you wake up the next day, you are pleasantly surprised to see a message on your phone that says your shipment has been dispatched. By noon, you get another message that your item is out for delivery. Today, customers want complete transparency in transactions, and the last mile of your delivery is the game changer.

Thankfully, for new advanced last-mile delivery software that can help iron out the creases, giving customers full control and visibility into the last mile delivery.

A last-mile delivery solution automates the time-consuming and repetitive tasks in the delivery process, saving a lot of time, resources and money for the customer and business. Manual methods of tracking such as waybills and handwritten-receipts or notes without barcodes are not only time consuming but also lead to human error. With the new modern last-mile delivery solution and technology, such systems become entirely automated, eliminating verification issues, and ensuring accurate and efficient load planning. These systems are designed to empower the customer and business with predictive insights.

Buyers are often looking for flexible delivery options, which add to the convenience of online shopping. For example, if you've ordered an urgently required medicine for your mom but might miss the parcel that's scheduled for delivery at your home address. Wouldn't it be great if you could visit the retailer's site and update your delivery time or address to either receive the parcel at a later time or have it delivered at your office address while you are there?

A last-mile delivery software makes this possible through real-time updates, allowing customers to change the time or location of deliveries with a tap, while also making it easier to handle cancellations and returns using the same system.

A last-mile delivery software can help by alerting you and your customers of any potential delays, leading to better expectation management and trust. Automatic delivery updates also keep customers updated of exact delivery times, ensuring their availability to accept the order and increasing the happiness score. **Welcome to the New World of Last Mile Logistics.**

Last Mile Delivery is Changing the World of Logistics

The New Word of Last Mile Logistics will never be the same. Let's start with last mile delivery companies and startups transforming shipping and same day delivery companies that's changing the game. I knew years ago that I wanted to be part of this exciting new changes in the logistics industry.

Based on my years of experience in the logistics industry, I know that legacy shippers don't have the capacity or network to quickly deliver parcels from their warehouses to the last mile. I have compiled a list of 13 startups and legacy logistics companies evolving to tackle e-commerce retailers' growing delivery problem.

Amazon, UPS and FedEx have dominated the US logistics industry—in particular, the last mile of delivery, where a courier brings a customer their order. FedEx estimates that more than 95% of all e-commerce orders in the US are delivered by itself, UPS, or the US Postal Service (USPS).

The Amazon Effect is Real, the Amazon Effect is the disruption to conventional physical retail locations caused by the increase in online shopping. ... Online shopping provides convenience and wide selection at often a good price.

Time has truly changed e-commerce sales—and customer expectations—are rising, leading to a surge in package volume. Legacy shippers don't have the capacity or network to quickly deliver parcels from their warehouses to the last mile. This has opened cracks in the space and presented a significant opportunity for last mile delivery startups to emerge.

From crowdsourcing to drones, here's how 13 legacy companies and startups are evolving to tackle e-commerce's growing delivery problem.

1. Amazon

Amazon presents the biggest near-term threat to the UPS and FedEx duopoly due to its size, innovation, and high level of consumer trust. Shipping is one of Amazon's highest costs, and it continues climbing every year as the e-commerce giant steadily builds out its logistics infrastructure and delivery network.

2. FedEx

FedEx offers door-to-door delivery service for time-sensitive packages through FedEx Same Day. Users can apply for accounts to use exclusively for same-day services 24/7/365 in all 50 US states. The logistics giant also offers Same Day Freight services for shipments greater than 150 lbs.

3. UPS

UPS standard ground and 2-day shipping, UPS provides a range of urgent and same-day delivery services with UPS Express Critical. Options include Air, Surface, Charter, Hand Carry, International, Secure, Inside Precision, and Value-Added Services depending on the sender's shipment needs.

4. XPO

XPO also offers expedited deliveries globally, and same-day courier services completing orders 24 hours a day, 364 days a year in the Tri-State areas of New York, New Jersey and Connecticut. XPOs courier service is comprised of uniformed employees, fleets of vehicles, and flexible options: same-day, next-day or pre-planned (routed and scheduled). For businesses employing their courier services, XPO offers customized engineering solutions, API/EDI connectivity for retail and e-commerce clients, and dedicated account managers.

5. USPS

The post office is lagging in same-day service for consumers, but offers Priority Mail Express, which comes with an Overnight Delivery Guarantee by 3pm (or earlier, if available, and at an additional charge).

For businesses, USPS does offer more robust same-day service through its The Last Mile Technologies experience. This suite of last mile solutions provides shipping transparency and efficiency "for business mailers and end-consumers alike" with intelligent scanning and documentation, real-time tracking, predictive delivery times, dynamic routing, and delivery performance analytics.

6. Walmart

Walmart has been steadily pushing into grocery delivery — and even tapping into self-driving vehicles for pilot programs in select locations. Same-day grocery customers can choose to pick their groceries up at a Walmart location for free. For in-store pickup, consumers order online, select a time slot, and Walmart employees will do all the in-store shopping and load their cars for them.

Same-day store pickup is available for some non-grocery items as well, and customers can track estimated arrival times and score in-store pickup discounts through the Walmart app.

7. Postmates

Postmates is a San Francisco-based urban logistics platform operating in 18 US cities that aims to enable "anyone to have anything delivered on-demand." The mobile platform is available as an iOS or Android app and connects customers with businesses and nearby couriers to place orders from local stores and restaurants.

8. Hitch

Tampa-based startup Hitch gives consumers, "the choice to be Shippers, Travelers, or both." The platform touts tapping into people power by pairing up shippers (the people placing the orders) with travelers (the local couriers) who are already heading in the direction that the item needs to go.

9. Darkstore

Darkstore is San Francisco-based urban fulfillment technology company operating in 40 US markets. Its key value proposition is Hosted Shopping Cart, which allows businesses to offer one hour delivery, same-day delivery, or standard shipping by adding just one line of code to their online checkout process.

10. ShipHawk

ShipHawk is a Santa Barbara-based SaaS company branding itself as the Smart Transportation Management System™ (TMS). Its transportation management and shipping software, TMS 2.0™, helps businesses save money, automate workflows, provide an on-brand buying experience, and run data-driven supply chains.

The all-in-one shipping intelligence solution offers multi-carrier rating, smart packing and order fulfillment, a carrier network for rate optimization, on-brand tracking, internal documentation, and detailed reporting and analytics to monitor carrier performance.

11. Narvar

San Francisco-based Narvar is focused on improving everything that happens after the Buy button. The platform enhances three aspects of the post-purchase phase of the customer journey: Convert by setting delivery expectations and communication preferences in cart, engage with customers by giving them branded experiences while they wait, and Care for the relationship by making the returns process seamless and easy.

Narvar uses machine learning to help businesses monitor interactions and understand customer trends. It integrates directly with e-commerce platforms, marketing tools, email service providers, and user-generated content, and leverages a network of more than 300 global carriers for fast, efficient delivery and returns.

12. Piggybee

Piggybee is a Brussels-based crowdshipping community. The service, which originally focused on European locations but has since expanded more globally, allows users to search for travelers much like they'd search for flights — by browsing departures and arrivals in different cities. Users also have the option to "post their trip" to request a delivery to a specific location.

When a user has found a traveler headed to their desired destination, they can message them to discuss purchase price and tip. In the spirit of travel, the service encourages users to consider trading accommodations, transport, or local advice in lieu of paying couriers a fee. After delivery, travelers are tipped through Piggybee MoneySafe, and rated.

13. Entrusters

Entrusters is an Argentina-based crowdshipping platform that touts "shopping without borders" to let consumers buy the best items at the best prices from abroad. It connects users to "Trusted Travelers" who use their extra luggage space to transport deliveries internationally.

Originally tied to Amazon, the platform has expanded to allow people to purchase items from any URL by selecting Buy It Now or requesting a delivery to their desired location. Like Piggybee, Entrusters encourages sharing authentic local experiences but, unlike Piggybee, its couriers can set delivery fees to help offset travel expenses.

My journey to becoming an Amazon Delivery Service Partner (DSP)

With over 30 years in Logistics Management, Supply Chain and Ownership with some of the largest companies in the world. I have had a front row seat to watching how Last Mile Delivery is Changing the World of Logistics.

So, when my wife Beverely Collier came home all excited after hearing about the Amazon Delivery Service Partner Program opportunity on a local radio station in 2018, I instantly knew that this was the right opportunity, and we are “Making History”.

I have participated in several DSP Recruiting Events, assisted with answering questions from potential new Amazon DSP's and I have been invited several times to Amazon HQ DSP Training in Seattle Washington to talk with new Delivery Service Partners and I was selected to become a member of Amazon DSP Community Advisory Group.

Let's Talk About How to Own Your Success

If you love building and leading teams, start your own business as an Amazon Delivery Service Partner, delivering smiles to customers across your community. I recommend that you Apply...

You bring leadership, Amazon will bring the rest. Amazon are looking for hands-on leaders who are passionate about hiring and coaching great teams. With low startup costs, built-in demand, and access to Amazon's technology and logistics experience, this is an opportunity to build and grow a successful package delivery business.

Amazon Delivery Service Partners in one of the fastest-growing industries in the world.

Let's Discuss the Amazon Advantage

- Low startup costs
- Start your business with as little as $10,000
- Logistics experience not required
- Use Amazon technology and processes
- Focus on people, not sales
- Amazon's packages keep your business growing, so you can focus on building a great team and delivering without worrying about driving sales.
- Support, when you need it

Amazon's experience is behind you every step of the way, from hands-on training to on-demand support to ensure your operation runs smoothly.

Delivering smiles is what we do, delight thousands of customers every day as an essential part of Amazon, the most customer-centric company on Earth.

Amazon is Committed to Diversity

Amazon have Diversity Grant to help reduce the barriers to entry for Black, Latinx, and Native American entrepreneurs—a $1 million commitment toward funding startup costs, offering $10,000 for each qualified candidate to build their own businesses in the U.S. With the launch of this grant program, Amazon investing in building a future for diverse business owners to serve their communities.

Are you a Great Leader?

If you are a great leader then this is a good program for you…….

Successful owners can expect:

- Annual revenue potential | $1M-4.5M
- Annual profit potential | $75K-300K

Startup costs are based on first 5 vans. Fully ramped partners operate 20-40 vans. Revenue and profit projections are for fully ramped partners. **Actual figures will vary...**

Is this the right opportunity for you?

If you're a customer-obsessed, hands-on leader who thrives in a high-speed, ever-changing environment, launching an Amazon Delivery Service Partner (DSP) business may be the opportunity for you. As a DSP owner, you'll focus on building a successful, safety-first work culture which includes recruitment, hiring and coaching a team of 40-100 high-performing, hourly employees and managing a fleet of 20-40 vans on average. Amazon will support you by providing a dedicated business coach and access to value-added services, such as uniforms and vehicle insurance, to help you run your business efficiently. With the right staffing and operational plan that allows you to adapt to demand throughout the year, you'll be set up to run a business that delivers packages 7 days a week, 361 days a year.

Great Team Leaders make great DSPs

The hardest part of being a successful owner is hiring, training, and managing a high-performing team. Owning a package delivery business takes strong leadership along with a lot of grit and hard work as you lead your team to deliver thousands of packages to happy customers every day. If that's your expertise, bring your leadership skills, and we will provide you with all of the technology and operational support you'll need.

Doing Your Homework on becoming an Amazon DSP

Let's talk about taking the next steps to become an Amazon Delivery Service Partner.

<u>What you need to know BEFORE you apply</u>

The success of the Amazon Delivery Service Program (DSP) is a reflection of its many owners. Their leadership, work ethic, and desire to give back to their communities are the foundation of our partnership. Being a DSP owner is hard work, and we want to make sure we partner with the right individuals. To allow candidates the ability to highlight their unique strengths and backgrounds, we have created an intensive selection process. The process is also lengthy due to the variability of our business and the high volume of interest. A journey from application to launch of your business may include the following experiences:

<u>Future DSP Program</u>

Currently, we invite most of our candidates who successfully pass their on-site interviews to join the Future DSP Program. The program offers onboarding and launch education ahead of a delivery station opening or becoming available. Future DSPs meet regularly with their Amazon Business Development Manager (BDM) to discuss questions and receive updates about locations. They also have the opportunity to learn from existing DSP owners on what to expect in our fast-paced, ever-changing environment, as well as advice on topics like building a high-performing team and coaching for customer obsession.

Ready to get started?

If you have the time, dedication, and qualifications to be a DSP owner, you are only three steps away from starting your journey.

First, determine if the location where you would like to operate is accepting applications. If your preferred location is not available, I encourage you to sign up to learn more about opportunity and program updates as they become available.

Second, after identifying your preferred location, take a deep breath and third and finally, create an account and get to work on submitting your application.

Step 1: Submit the Online Application

Step 2: Complete the Candidate Screening Process

Step 3: Join the Future DSP Program (Invite Only)

Step 4: Receive a Rate Pay Card and Offer (Based on Location Availability)

Step 5: Complete Two (2) Weeks of Hands-on Training

Step 6: Setup your Business and Build a Team

Step 7: Start Operating Your Business (Welcome to the DSP Family)

Let's Talk About Your Rules of Engagement - What you do?

- Set up your business

Amazon provide and connect you with a suite of deals to acquire the assets you need to start your business, and work with the network of service providers to keep your business rolling.

- Build your team

You're a coach. This is your team. As you set up your business, the most important step you'll take is recruiting and retaining solid drivers who will enable the ongoing success of your operation.

- Deliver packages

You will manage a fleet of 20-40 vans on average per day. Serving thousands of customers daily isn't easy, but the smiles are incredibly rewarding.

- Create your team culture

Your can-do attitude ensures your business reflects Amazon's high standards and customer-obsessed culture. Motivate your team to exceed expectations on every delivery through coaching and development.

- Grow your business

Deliver a great customer experience to gain more opportunities to hire more people and deliver additional packages to further grow your business.

Let's Discuss Amazon Rules of Engagement - What Amazon do?

- Get you started

Amazon exclusive deals on Amazon-branded vans, comprehensive insurance, industrial-grade handheld devices, and other services help you get your delivery business up and running.

- Provide training

Amazon provide two weeks of hands-on training to ensure you're set up for success, starting with a one-week virtual classroom introduction to Amazon, followed by one week in a delivery station working with a community of existing owners and drivers to learn the tips and tricks of operating a successful delivery business from those who know it best. All in-person trainings incorporate social distancing and enhanced safety measures.

The Best Industry Training

Week 1 of Training | Your introduction to Amazon and starting your business

- Discover Amazon's customer-obsessed culture
- Receive valuable advice on setting up a new business from an expert
- Deep dive all the exclusive deals that Amazon has negotiated for you
- Master the best practices of hiring, training, and engaging a large team of employees
- Learn more about the ins and outs of running a delivery business

Week 2 of Training | In the field—learn how to become a successful Amazon Delivery Service Partner

- Observe the daily processes at an Amazon delivery station

- Assist in sorting and loading out Amazon packages
- Work alongside existing DSP owners to watch their dispatch and on-road management in action
- Learn about the tools used to manage a delivery business
- Get acquainted with delivery station personnel
- Troubleshoot common issues that your drivers and helpers may face on the road
- Debrief with station personnel after each day of deliveries, and gather tips and tricks on ways to improve delivery quality, safety, and efficiency
- Give you a comprehensive toolkit

Amazon give you all the tools and technology you'll need to run your business, including daily processes designed to keep your operation running smoothly.

- Offer on-demand support

Owners receive ongoing support from Amazon, which includes a comprehensive operation manual, driver assistance for on-road issues, and a dedicated Business Coach.

- Share their experience

Amazon shares more than 20 years of technological and logistics experience to guide you in one of the fastest-growing industries in the world.

At the End of the Day - What you'll need?

- Customer obsession

You start with the customer and work backwards.

- Leadership

You love people! You are great at leading and retaining a team of drivers.

- Deliver results

Your can-do attitude inspires your team to handle labor-intensive delivery work, even when challenges arise.

- Resilience

You're capable of dealing with the ambiguity of a fast-paced, ever-changing business.

FAQ's |Program Details

What should I consider before applying to Amazon's Delivery Service Partner (DSP) program?

This opportunity is a good fit for those who are looking to run a full-time business, have experience hiring and coaching teams, and are comfortable in a fast-paced, ever-changing environment. Running a package-delivery business is hard work and requires DSP owners to hire, train, develop, and retain a team of 40-100 employees, and manage a fleet of 20-40 vans on average. We are looking for candidates who love building and growing a team, have the grit and leadership required to roll up their sleeves to get work done, enjoy operating as a part of a larger community, and have a can-do attitude that inspires their team to handle labor-intensive delivery work. We look at a wide range of information on each applicant, including work history, education, and financial information, to determine eligibility for the program.

Please note this is a lengthy and highly competitive selection process with limited available openings. Most candidates that pass an on-site interview will be invited to join the Future DSP Program until a station opens or becomes available. Future DSPs meet regularly with their Amazon Business Development Manager and receive educational materials to help them understand the launch processes and expectations. While an offer is not guaranteed, engaged Future DSPs are notified about local opportunities first.

This opportunity may not be a good fit for those looking to make a passive investment, work part-time, or run a package-delivery business in multiple locations/regions. Applicants who indicate they have relationships with persons or entities that pose a conflict of interest are ineligible to be a Delivery

Service Partner (DSP). For example, any person with an interest (equity, financial, debt, contract, or other) in a DSP business may not have an interest in any other DSP business. Additionally, DSPs may not have a spouse or partner with an existing DSP business.

If you feel that you are a good fit, we encourage you to request information here to learn more.

How many vans can I expect to operate at any given time?

As a DSP owner, you can expect to manage a fleet of 20-40 vans on average throughout the year. The number of vans you manage depends on many factors, including the volume of packages at the delivery station, your performance and safety record, and your compliance with program guidelines. The volume of packages at a delivery station will fluctuate based upon customer purchasing behaviors, busy shopping periods like Prime Day or the holidays, and other factors. To help you plan for these changes in package volume, Amazon works with you to provide advance notice as we anticipate these changes. In our experience, the most successful DSP owners adapt to these variables by setting up their teams in a manner that lets them increase or decrease staffing, vans, and other business operations based on demand.

Are there any resources available to learn more about the program?

We encourage you to attend one of our webinars for more information about the program. As you progress in the application process, you will have a chance to attend other webinars with current Amazon Delivery Service Partner owner-operators and Amazon Business Development Managers to address your specific questions. In addition, qualified candidates who have passed their interviews may have the opportunity to visit Amazon delivery stations, meet with Amazon employees, and learn more about the specifics of owning and operating a delivery business.

Locations/Expansion

For which locations are you seeking applications?

Amazon community of DSPs operates in cities throughout the United States. Amazon are currently looking to review applications of candidates interested in these areas. If your location of choice does not appear in this list, then we encourage you to sign up to learn more and receive updates about new opportunities as they become available. If you are seeking opportunities outside the United States, please see below for more information.

What are your plans to expand the program into other cities?

Amazon are continually growing this program to empower more entrepreneurs to create jobs and deliver for their communities. Amazon are expanding our delivery services and infrastructure in areas where we have sufficient package volume to support the work of DSP companies. Amazon encourage anyone with interest to apply so that they can be first to select their location of choice when it's available. You will be invited to interview when we have available openings in your area.

Do you offer the DSP program in other countries?

The DSP program is currently available in other countries and expanding into others.

- Canada

- United Kingdom
- Spain
- Germany
- Itay
- Ireland
- Brazil
- India

I want to be able to do the program in multiple cities – is that possible?

The program is currently designed for owners to operate delivery businesses within a single delivery station with fleets of 20-40 vans on average throughout the year. Although we are unable to comment on the future of the program at this time, we can say that we're committed to helping owners grow a successful business delivering packages in their community.

Value added services

Can you provide details of value-added services offered by Amazon?

Amazon have secured exclusive deals to get your business up and running with low upfront costs. These include branded Amazon vans customized for delivery, fuel program, high quality branded uniforms, rugged devices, and business services such as recruiting tool discounts, payroll, tax & accounting software discounts, legal support, and insurance options.

I have an existing fleet of vans; can I use those to run my delivery business with Amazon?

The Delivery Service Partner is responsible for procuring delivery vehicles for its operations. Amazon has negotiated a "flexible lease" option that enables you to lease Amazon-branded vans designed specifically for this program from a third-party fleet management company. However, if you already have a pre-existing fleet of vehicles, you certainly can use them if the vehicles meet our requirements. Complete vehicle specification requirements will be shared later in the application process.

Financials

How much start-up capital is required and are there any unexpected costs I should account for?

Assuming that you choose to take advantage of all third-party deals impacting startup costs that have been negotiated by Amazon in connection with the program, we estimate that it will cost DSP owners $10,000 to start their businesses. This is not a fee paid to Amazon, but represents our estimate of what it will cost to cover key startup costs including legal entity formation and licensing, professional services like accountant and lawyer fees, set up supplies such as a laptop and timekeeping software, recruiting costs such as job postings, drug tests, and driver training, and your travel for owner training. Upfront costs for delivery vehicles are excluded from our estimate as there is no upfront cost for delivery vehicles procured through the delivery vehicle leasing program negotiated by Amazon.

Can you help me better understand the financials of this opportunity?

As the potential business owner, you will be responsible for seeking out detailed financial information and building your own profit and loss statement and/or cost model. As you progress through the application process, you'll learn more specifics about the business and associated costs – especially the costs of exclusive deals and discounts negotiated by Amazon for Delivery Service Partners. We recommend that you start by reviewing the program brochure which includes a breakdown of the types of costs that you can expect your company to incur. From there, you can conduct your own research on these costs specific to your location in order to model an expected profit and loss statement. Over time, you can refine the profit and loss statement to better understand the financial implications of the program.

If the start-up cost is estimated to be $10,000, why is the liquid asset requirement $30,000?

The application requires that you submit documentation demonstrating access to $30,000 in liquid assets. This ensures you have sufficient funds to cover both the estimated business startup costs of $10,000 and to cover your personal expenses while you are training and launching your business.

Application Process

What are the steps involved in completing the application?

Candidates first submit an online application that requests information about previous work experience, leadership, financial health, community involvement, and geographic preferences, as well as a credit check, background screening and motor vehicle record check. If selected to progress for further consideration, next steps include a screening interview, an opportunity to ask questions of a current Amazon DSP owner via live webinar, and then a final round of virtual interviews. Once Amazon provides an offer to become a DSP, candidates will have the opportunity to discuss specific details about the station, routes, and financials before a final decision is made.

Candidates will receive updates and timelines based on their geographic location and other factors to the email associated with their account.

What screening criteria do you use in selecting DSP candidates?

Strong financial acumen, people management, and recruiting skills are critical to the success of a DSP. Therefore, we look for candidates who will be hands-on owner-operators and can demonstrate experience managing a budget or profit and loss statement, a strong credit report, and ability to hire, motivate, and manage teams of employees. No previous logistics experience is required. We find that candidates who are active and involved in their communities are often most successful in hiring drivers for their businesses. Therefore, please include any community involvement in your application.

Only one applicant may apply. Applicants who indicate they have relationships with persons or entities that pose a conflict of interest are ineligible to be a Delivery Service Partner (DSP). For example, any person with an interest (equity, financial, debt, contract, or other) in a DSP business may not have an interest in any other DSP business. Additionally, DSPs may not have a spouse or partner with an existing DSP business.

Candidates are required to pass a background check, which includes a motor vehicle record check, credit check, recorded screening interview based on questions focused on the Amazon Leadership Principles. Additionally, $30,000 in liquid assets in an approved bank account are required to starting the business. We encourage you to refer to our application tips document when completing your application.

Get familiar with your financial history by checking your credit report for free from Experian. You're entitled to one free report per year from each of the three credit reporting agencies—Equifax, Experian and TransUnion—which you can access on AnnualCreditReport.com. Learn more about credit scores here.

What information and documents should I have available while filling out the application?

As you begin the application process, please review these tips and have the following information available:

- Personal information and an up-to-date resume

- Full work history, including dates of employment and current income information

- Full military service information, if applicable

- Full educational history, including dates of attendance and GPAs

- Personal financial information, including assets and liabilities

Can I apply and operate as a DSP Owner with one or more partners?

Only one person may apply in a given application to become a Delivery Service Partner (DSP) owner. We do not accept applications from companies or groups and may disqualify applicants who indicate they have relationships with persons or entities that pose conflicts of interest.

During the interview process, only the applicant will be interviewed; thus, the applicant's experience and strategies must be able to address all interview questions. If accepted into the program, the owner will sign the DSP Agreement and will be required to attend all trainings. The owner may elect to hire and train other partners as needed, but the owner will remain the main point of contact for Amazon delivery station leaders and Business Coaches. Additionally, applicants who indicate they have relationships with persons or entities that pose a conflict of interest are ineligible to be a Delivery Service Partner (DSP). For example, any person with an interest (equity, financial, debt, contract, or other) in a DSP business may not have an interest in any other DSP business. Additionally, DSPs may not have a spouse or partner with an existing DSP business.

I need to make edits to my application. How do I do that?

Before submitting the application, you can go into the application portal at any time to make edits. Unfortunately, once you have submitted your application you will not be able to make any changes to it. Therefore, we recommend reviewing your application thoroughly before submitting it.

I am unable to submit my application. What do I do now?

If you're experiencing an issue submitting your application, we recommend that you save your application and try logging out, logging in again, and then submit the application. If that doesn't work, please contact support by emailing Amazon.

I have submitted my application. What happens now?

We will review your application and get back to you as soon as possible. Please note that this is a highly competitive program with a limited number of available openings; therefore, it might take us months before we are able to get back to you on your application. The email address that you use to apply will be our primary contact method to inform you of your status and next steps.

How do I check the status of my application?

You can log into the application portal to view the status of your application. If and when your application status updates, you'll also receive an email informing you of the updated status.

Future DSP Program

What is the Future DSP Program?

Candidates who successfully pass the on-site interview will likely be invited to join the Future DSP Program. The program offers onboarding and launch education ahead of a delivery station opening or becoming available. Future DSPs meet regularly with their Amazon Business Development Manager to answer questions and provide location updates. They also have the opportunity to learn more from existing DSPs on what to expect in our fast paced, ever-changing environment as well as receive advice on topics like building a high performing team and coaching for customer obsession.

When will I know if I will be invited to join the Future DSP Program?

Amazon aim to notify candidates prior to their on-site interview. However, the program evolves rapidly, so there will be cases where an update is not available until after the on-site interview.

How long will I be a Future DSP?

The timing of an opportunity is based on location availability and if there are other Future DSPs already interested in the same location. While we cannot offer a timeline, we can commit to providing frequent, and transparent updates.

Am I guaranteed an offer as a Future DSP?

No, at this time, no offer is guaranteed to any Future DSP.

Should I quit my job to be a Future DSP?

No, the education offered to Future DSPs is self-paced and accessible online. Therefore, there is no need to leave current employment to be in the Future DSP program. Timelines for becoming a DSP owner and associations with other employment are discussed at the time of offer and signing of the program agreement.

What are the benefits of the Future DSP Program?

Future DSPs have exclusive access to resources to help set them up for success. They meet regularly with their designated Amazon Business Development Manager and receive educational modules on how to prepare for launch and what to expect.

Why apply now to be a Future DSP?

Engaged Future DSPs have a place on the interest list for their location of preference, and therefore, when an opportunity arises, Business Development Managers reach out to them first. Also, the onboarding time can be as short as 7 weeks. Future DSPs have more time to educate themselves with the launch processes and expectations.

Let's Talk About Last Mile Delivery Industry

I have provided you with the Steps to becoming an Amazon Delivery Partner, NOW let's talk about what's last mile delivery.

<u>What is Last Mile Delivery?</u>

The last mile refers to the final step in the supply chain, when a product transfers from a business (typically a retail store, warehouse, or distribution center) to the customer's business or home, or to a collection point, like an ecommerce lockbox.

The focus of last mile logistics is to deliver items to the end user as fast as possible. While it seems simple enough, the last mile is an expensive mile, in fact it is by far the most expensive part of the fulfillment chain.

Until the boom in ecommerce, most last mile deliveries consisted of consumer and business goods moving on pallets from manufacturing plants, warehouses, or distribution centers to other businesses or retail stores. The participants in these supply chains became adept at moving large volumes of products quickly and efficiently.

In contrast, the last mile in ecommerce deliveries involves numerous small orders going to different locations. This drives up the expense of the last mile. Business Insider estimates it accounts for more than half — 53 percent — of total shipping costs.

The growth in ecommerce over the past year has magnified last mile challenges. In Canada, 2020 ecommerce sales were expected to hit CA$52.04 billion, up more than 20 percent from 2019, according to Insider Intelligence. Ecommerce sales in the U.S. during 2020 were estimated at US$791.7 billion, up nearly one-third from 2019.

Estimated Quarterly U.S Retail E-Commerce Sales

While the challenges that accompany the last mile of any delivery are daunting, organizations that figure out how to effectively tackle them can boost customer satisfaction, rein in costs, and gain a competitive advantage. Consider that more than half — 55 percent — of consumers will shift to competitors that offers faster delivery.

Just as important, manufacturers and brands that become adept at handling the last mile can build direct relationships with their customers. "Rather than rely entirely on wholesalers and retailers, you can reshape your customers' experiences more closely to your brand.

An efficient, reliable, last mile function will become even more critical as the volume of final mile deliveries grow. The last mile delivery market in North America is forecast to grow by US$44.88 billion between 2020 and 2024, for a compound annual growth rate that tops 14 percent, Technavio reports.

Customers Last Mile Delivery Challenges and Opportunities

It is precisely at the last mile that many incumbent logistics providers are struggling, and these businesses are at a competitive disadvantage as new companies disrupt the market with innovative business models that address customer demand for ever-faster delivery.

While tackling end mile delivery challenges is a daunting undertaking, companies that wait or ignore this function risk losing business to competitors that act more quickly. "Companies needs a last mile delivery strategy that's tailored and customized to their needs. Customization is key, as many last mile challenges and opportunities vary by industry.

Brick and Mortar Retailers

Brick and mortar retailers typically operate stores that are scattered across a region or even a country — as well as warehouses and distribution centers that keep those stores stocked. Most warehouses have been built to move cases and pallets of items with precision and efficiency.

Now, however, the growing volume of online orders upends this traditional business model. While many retailers still need to ensure their stores offer an array of goods, they also need to gain competency in filling the single orders that come with online sales, a vastly different packing and fulfillment process than working with cases or pallets. Those that don't risk losing customers. For instance, 53 percent of customers say speed of delivery is the most important factor when it comes to fulfillment of online orders.

Brick and Mortar Retailers - Last Mile Delivery

At the same time, stores provide an advantage, as they enable you to hold inventory close to your customers, whether they're shopping on site or online. As a result, same-day local delivery becomes more feasible. More than 50 percent of ecommerce purchases will be delivered from local inventory — and that number could easily be 70 percent.

Some retailers, particularly in the grocery space, are turning a portion of their stores into fulfillment centers for online orders—generally, a less expensive option than adding new warehouse space. Real estate firm CBRE writes, "More traditional grocery store formats and specialty players, especially in urban and more densely populated areas, will shift store space toward distribution uses..."

Ecommerce Only Retailers

The last mile delivery challenges shift a bit for ecommerce only retailers. Their warehouses and fulfillment centers typically are, of course, tailored to filling ecommerce orders. However, many uses postal services or traditional carriers to fill orders. That can mean a less than optimal customer experience. Many traditional carriers are experts at transporting items over long stretches of road. These carriers may be less adept at meeting timelines for local deliveries or handling larger and bulkier items. When a delivery does not meet expectations, customers typically blame the company from which they ordered, rather than the delivery company.

In addition, consumers, including business-to-business buyers, judge ecommerce retailers by the leaders in the space — what I call the "**Amazonification**" of consumers' expectations. Deliveries need to be quick, efficient, accurate, ideally at low cost, all while allowing customers to track their orders every step of the way.

Manufacturing (B2B + B2C)

Manufacturers have traditionally reached their customers through retailers and wholesalers. While these models are unlikely to disappear any time soon, many manufacturers now can also transact directly with their customers. The benefits? The ability to strengthen these relationships by communicating directly with promotions, news, and new products. Manufacturers that maintain histories of customers' purchases can tailor their communication to fit each customer.

Company delivery model is a key factor that will determine the success of your efforts to reach consumers directly. It needs to be reliable, quick, cost effective, and scalable, what **I call the "Amazonification"**. Not all delivery firms can deliver — pardon the pun — these qualities. On the other hand, building your own fleet is costly. Company organization has to incur the expense not only of the initial fleet purchase, but also its ongoing operations and maintenance costs. It's also difficult to rapidly scale an in-house fleet. Furthermore, building an in-house fleet diverts management's attention from the organization's core objectives.

Moreover, not even the largest companies can afford fleets capable of handling all their delivery needs. Despite a sizeable investment, they still risk insufficient delivery capacity and disappointed customers.

B2B Suppliers

While much of the attention around ecommerce has centered on the rapidly growing numbers of consumers ordering online, business-to-business (B2B) transactions are also increasing. Today, business recipients account for almost half of parcel deliveries, Lux Research reports. Many business customers assume that purchasing products for their business operations should be just as streamlined as ordering the latest best seller or a new pair of shoes.

While some suppliers invest in their own vehicle fleets, they often run up against the same challenges as businesses that build fleets dedicated to consumer orders, including steep initial investments and sizable ongoing expenses. Management must allocate attention and resources to the fleet, rather than the organization's goals. Moreover, even companies that make this investment can rarely meet every delivery need, and so they still risk disappointed customers.

Technology and Innovative Solutions Help Last Mile Delivery Logistics

Technology can help overcome some of the final mile delivery challenges faced by retailers, suppliers, and manufacturers. In fact, Lux Research predicts automated delivery technologies, including drones, autonomous vehicles, and robots will generate between $33 and $48 billion in annual delivery revenues by 2030, even though they'll deliver less than 20 percent of parcels.

Micro-Fulfillment Through Malls + Storefronts

Another option for last mile fulfillment and delivery is to use malls and/or storefronts as micro-fulfillment centers. More than half — 57 percent — of retailers prefer using their retail stores to fill orders with two-hour delivery timeframes, and more than 40 percent prefer to use retail backrooms for same-day delivery, CapGemini found.

By using stores and malls as distribution centers, firms leverage their existing assets. Just as important, these properties typically are located near their customer base, facilitating speedier deliveries.

Some new solutions enable customers to shop an entire mall from their computer and then receive all their purchases in one delivery stop. This more closely replicates the in-person experience of shopping and makes for a more efficient delivery experience.

Smart Tracking and Route Optimization

Along with advances in hardware, software is evolving to better handle last mile deliveries. Smart tracking and route optimization solutions can help companies boost the efficiency with which they complete deliveries. These solutions often leverage technologies like artificial intelligence and machine learning to optimize routes and reduce delays.

Drones

While drones may still sound futuristic, researchers at the University of Texas at Dallas say the technology offers the potential to be a genuine game changer by speeding last mile deliveries, while also allowing them to occur hands-free — critical in a post-pandemic era. They predict that both the number of last-mile warehouses and delivery speed of drones will increase as the technology matures, leading to decentralized last mile delivery networks. These two shifts will work together, as the increasing speed of drones really becomes helpful only when accompanied by an increase in last-mile warehouses.

Drones also may be especially useful in rural areas, where the distance between delivery points adds expense. In addition, they're well-suited to transporting - but high-value items, like many medicines.

These benefits are driving a compound annual growth rate of 38.5 percent in the drone delivery market, which is expected to reach US$2.2 billion in 2025, according to Business Research Company.

Electric Vehicles

Electric vehicles are another delivery option, particularly in densely populated urban areas. Electric vehicles can reduce spending on fuel and maintenance, enhance driver safety, and are environmentally friendly.

As more customers look for brands to make sustainable choices, electric vehicles can be an appealing option for companies looking to invest in the emerging green logistics marketplace.

Wheeled Robots

Wheeled robots that can travel at about five miles per hour have been tried on college campuses for several years, Lux Research reports. These machines can carry several packages at a time and operate on sidewalks, rather than roads. A small, but slowly growing number of entities are allowing their use. In November 2020, for instance, Pennsylvania passed legislation allowing some personal delivery devices — another term for wheeled robots — to use the sidewalks.

Parcel Lockers

Another option is bringing delivery items to parcel lockers from which consumers pick up their deliveries. The Urban Freight Lab at the University of Washington Supply Chain Transportation and Logistics Center found parcel lockers in a traditional office building reduced total delivery time by 78 percent. Even better, no deliveries failed. While lockers might not always slash delivery time by such a large magnitude, the study showed the potential benefits.

Partnering with a Last Mile Delivery Transportation Company

As customer expectations for delivery continue to rise, companies need to take a hard look at how they can meet (or exceed) those expectations to stay competitive. Orders must be delivered to satisfaction every single time — regardless of location or time of year.

Without the right last mile partner, most companies will struggle to deliver same day or faster consistently. And the risks of disappointing customers are high. 84 percent of customers won't return after a single bad delivery experience, making it table stakes to deliver on time, every time.

By partnering with the right last-mile delivery partner, you can ensure your deliveries are on time, reliable, and appropriately reflect your brand, even during the busiest holiday seasons.

How to Choose a Last Mile Delivery Partner

When choosing a last mile partner, the following questions can help you decide if a company is a fit:

- Scalability: Can the company's solution stay at or ahead of your company's growth?
- Service Levels: Will the company commit to meeting your expectations for delivery speed and accuracy?
- Professionalism: Are the drivers trained professionals that will represent your brand appropriately?
- Accountability. How does the company ensure customer satisfaction? For instance, do they monitor and track customer reviews? What reporting capabilities does the firm offer?

- Technology: Can the company meet your customers' expectations for real-time tracking and notifications, predictable pricing, analytics, and other technical capabilities?
- Partnership: Will your firm be partnered with an expert at the firm who knows your business? Or will you simply be one of many clients?

Conclusion The Bottomline

To be sure, optimizing last mile deliveries remains a complex undertaking that likely will become even more so, given increasing customer expectations, growing ecommerce sales, and advancing technology. However, companies must address these challenges now to hold onto their customers and remain competitive.

Partnering with an innovative, reliable last-mile company that provides outstanding service tailored to your needs, can help your business meet these challenges. You'll be able to control expenses, strengthen client relationships, and drive sustained success.

Most importantly, you'll be able to deliver exactly when customers want, every single day of the year.

New Rules for Last Mile Delivery in the eCommerce Era

Last mile delivery has become one of the most important concepts on the frequently changing and emerging eCommerce stage. "Traditional" supply chain management is being turned on its head by consumer demands for more options, and increased expectations around the last mile experience.

Understanding last mile delivery and its role in effect on customer satisfaction is critical to every business today, from global enterprise to smaller e-commerce sellers. Companies that are looking further down the road, are already identifying and implementing last mile logistics solutions to help them compete with the giants of eCommerce.

In this guide, we'll discuss the latest trends in last mile delivery, how they are impacting businesses, and the capabilities you need to create a competitive customer experience.

Why is last mile delivery important?

eCommerce has become an increasingly larger percent of retail sales, causing eCommerce fulfillment in general, and last mile delivery in particular, to become a mission-critical arena for brands and the logistics providers who deliver for them.

In Q3 of 2020, almost $1 in $5 spent was online, with almost 50% of U.S. shoppers doing most of their shopping online.

The COVID 19 pandemic threw eCommerce ages forward with almost no advanced notice. eCommerce growth expected to take the next 5-10 years occurred within 6-12 months, bringing with it a major hurdle for online sellers: the eCommerce fulfillment process.

Spurred on by rising consumer expectations for faster delivery and more convenient options, major players in the industry are setting new expectations for fulfillment speed, cost and convenience. This increased competition means that retailers and marketplaces need to step up and improve their logistics operations and last mile delivery services. However, operational costs can be prohibitive, and shipping companies are struggling to keep up with record-breaking demand. Solving these challenges will to a large degree define whether retailers and other eCommerce players will successfully scale their online sales.

Major trends in last mile delivery

Home delivery is growing rapidly

With the boom in eCommerce, home deliveries are increasing rapidly and presenting new and unique challenges for last mile logistics providers. Shipping companies must keep up with increasing consumer demands and meet high expectations in order to keep both retailers and parcel recipients satisfied with services.

Contactless and white glove delivery

Convenience and safety are two of the major areas that retailers must emphasize in their last mile delivery process today, which is why many companies have started offering premium services, such as white glove delivery. This is usually available for high-ticket items or physically large items and can include delivery and installation or assembly in the correct room of your house.

Contactless delivery – Many customers prefer to have contactless fulfillment options. Offering to drop off packages at the customer's doorstep and other contactless delivery processes may boost brand loyalty and be a new customer magnet for those looking for this option.

What is last mile delivery, and how does it work?

Last mile delivery, also known as final mile delivery, is the last leg of the supply chain – the handoff between the business and the end customer.

There are five main steps to the primary last mile delivery flow:

- Online orders are processed through a centralized system. This gives both the sender and the recipient the ability to track and understand where the order is on the supply chain.
- The order makes its way and arrives at the transportation hub.
- Packages are dispatched to a specific fleet or vehicle, which is assigned a route. This process can be automated (in the case of on demand delivery), manual, or a combination of the two.
- Orders are scanned when leaving the transportation hub in order to keep the system – and all stakeholders – updated along the last mile.
- The package arrives at the final delivery destination and the delivery attempt is confirmed.

Types of last mile delivery

There are two main types of last mile delivery: scheduled and on-demand.

Scheduled is when a customer places an order to be delivered the next day, two days later or even a week later. On-demand delivery is when an order must be delivered the same day or even ASAP (such as food and restaurant delivery).

In last mile delivery, customer experience is everything

eCommerce competition is vast and constantly expanding. To maintain customer loyalty, brands and last mile logistics providers must invest in an exceptional delivery experience. In particular, same day delivery has become a "must" in order to keep customer loyalty high.

Take Amazon, for example. In addition to one-day shipping, the eCommerce behemoth maintained its competitive advantage by coming out with 2-hour delivery on certain products for Prime subscribers, pushing the boundaries of fast delivery.

We already know that customers love brands who offer same day delivery. In fact, 57% of customers say that same day delivery will make them more loyal to a specific brand. So why isn't everyone doing it?

The answer is simple: costs. Last mile logistics and fast delivery are so expensive, that Amazon decided it would be more cost-effective to build its own supply chain.

The exact order fulfillment models that consumers demand is also the most costly for retailers and their logistics partners to implement.

Running the last mile delivery process through both internal and external fleets

Companies which need to deliver goods use either an 'owned' fleet, third party providers, or a combination of the two.

Internal fleets or 'owned' fleets are run and dispatched internally within a company. Internal fleets have an advantage of being easily accessible and flexible to use.

External fleets refer to third party delivery providers, including crowdsourced fleets, 3PL logistics companies, and shipping carriers. Today companies often turn to third party carriers when their own fleet can't handle the last mile volume anymore, or if they don't want the burden of managing the process themselves.

The challenges of last mile logistics

As the shift from brick and mortar to online retail continues, new customer expectations regarding last mile fulfillment speed, convenience and costs have strengthened existing challenges for online retailers and logistics providers.

These logistics challenges fall into four main categories:

Speed

One Incisive report showed that 84% of surveyed shoppers ranked speed of pickup for "buy online pickup in-store" or curbside orders to be very important. In an American Express and Forrester survey, 57% of respondents stated that same-day shipping would make them more loyal to a customer's brand.

Still, speed is not as critical of an issue today as it was in the past. Safety and convenience have taken the lead as top priorities for customers. Price, as always, is another major consideration. Many customers prefer to wait another day for free shipping rather than pay 5 or 10 dollars for same-day shipping. By offering flexible choices, customers are able to choose if speed, price or other considerations are their priority.

Businesses may have an advantage by delivering faster as this will reduce their cost to deliver and, as a byproduct, their shipping prices. Also, the faster that orders get delivered, the sooner capacity is opened up, enabling more deliveries with the same amount of resources.

Visibility

Last mile delivery anxiety is the stress consignees feel when they don't know where their order is, or when it is arriving – and it's become a serious concern for brands and ecommerce sellers.

In the era of on-demand everything, tracking codes are no longer enough. Shippers and end customers want and expect full, real-time tracking with their order: to see where the driver is at any given moment and exactly when he or she will arrive.

Efficiency

Customers today expect fast delivery that requires efficient last mile logistics processes. One method of increasing efficiency is to make sure that vehicles maximize load capacity. Take, for example, a mattress company with an order to ship 20 mattresses, but a truck which can only manage 5 mattresses at a time. The driver has to perform several runs back and forth between warehouse and end location to complete a single order. The cost of gas is greater than if a more appropriate vehicle had been assigned to that order. This is an example of an inefficient last mile process.

This inefficiency costs both logistics companies and retailers' large sums of money. The same goes for dispatchers who manually plan routes, the call centers that have to deal with unhappy or confused customers and more. As soon as the process becomes efficient, everybody wins.

For both retailers and logistics companies, efficiency is also critical to increasing order fulfillment capacity. When lacking efficiency, large order volumes can cause your services to veer off schedule and lead to late or failed deliveries and annoyed customers.

This is where technology can make a difference. Innovative logistics management software allows retailers to automate traditionally manual processes: from deciding where to fulfill orders from, to dispatching orders to different fleets or drivers across multiple geographic locations based on multiple variables.

Managing a last mile delivery service provider

Today, 3 out of 4 retailers expect to work with third party fleets, often in combination with an in-house fleet. Being able to manage drivers from third party sources on the same dashboard and through the same system as your own fleet is crucial for scaling last mile delivery operations.

When planning order fulfillment, evaluating and choosing the best last mile carrier or 3PL for your business is of the utmost importance. At the end of the day, the carrier is the face of your brand when it finally meets your customer. It is important to evaluate a last mile delivery service provider based on your specific needs and have access to operational and commerce performance in order to effectively compare logistics providers.

On demand vs. scheduled deliveries

Efficiency also means different things for on demand and scheduled deliveries:

Planned deliveries – Planned deliveries typically fit a highly specialized cadence. For example, one type of planned delivery might require that any orders for next-day delivery be placed by noon. Dispatchers would review the next day's deliveries at noon, often with the help of automated route optimization software. There are numerous variables to be taken into account, including driver ratings, driver certifications (e.g., licensed for cable installation), inventory availability, transit time, parking availability, time-on-site, vehicle type and vehicle capacity. To take more variables into account requires a dedicated technology.

Whereas manual routing typically takes dispatchers a few hours, an intelligent route planner app can provide a fully optimized route within minutes. Many dispatchers will then further optimize these routes based on their personal knowledge of the business, the drivers and the local geography. When drivers arrive the next morning, they are given their runs so they can begin their day's work.

Same day delivery – on demand delivery comes with its own set of problems to tackle, revolving mostly around lack of time and the costs involved.

- Lack of planning: with ASAP orders, dispatching and mapping routes must be done automatically, otherwise it is essentially impossible to optimize for speed and cost.
- Managing customer expectations: There's no time for customers to make changes such as delivery location or even a change in the order.
- Costs: Sending out a delivery to one person is typically not highly cost-effective. You don't have time to figure out what goes in each vehicle, and how to organize to get each delivery out and to its destination in the shortest amount of time possible and with the smallest use of resources, unless you are digitized and automated.

Dealing with exceptions

Every on-demand fulfillment model needs to include the ability to efficiently manage delivery exceptions, such as:

- An order that includes an out-of-stock item
- An order is not staged on time, so it is not ready when the truck is due to leave
- A customer requests a change in the delivery time or address
- A previous delivery, particularly a service delivery, cannot be completed on time, delaying the next service appointment
- A failed or missed delivery
- The customer rejects part of the order due to missing or faulty products

Each of these issues can have an impact on every other function in the last mile delivery process, as well as on the customer.

Driver efficiency and churn

Investing in optimized routes and other efficiency tech is worthless if there is no compliance from the drivers. For this reason (among others), the ability to track where all drivers are at any given time is tied with greater operational efficiency. A centralized system that tracks driver location in real time helps businesses keep track of their drivers, understand issues in performance, and see whether their tech solutions are being utilized.

Logistics providers can also tackle driver churn through a mobile app for drivers that helps them manage their routes and all the requirements per order. This makes the driver's work easier, and also allows them to complete more orders per run.

Cost

According to some estimates, 28% of the total delivery cost to a business comes from the last mile. Too often, companies pass these costs on to the customer. Combine the issue of cost with the heightened expectations for same day or on-demand delivery, and you have a recipe for strain on budgets and logistics providers.

Additionally, retailers often find their last mile delivery costs soaring when they haven't properly planned for inconsistent demand – for example, during peak seasons or peak times of day. All of this makes it challenging to run delivery profitably.

Owning the entire supply chain is not a viable option for most businesses, and there is no one solution to cut costs for last mile deliveries. However, proper planning, and optimizing your supply chain through technology can go a long way to reducing some of these expenses.

The bottom line: efficient operations is a must for meeting demand

Growing demand should be a blessing for any business. But while the rise in eCommerce is a welcome transition for many online sellers, scaling up delivery services efficiently and quickly can be daunting.

Without an efficient supply chain and operations system in place, businesses will find themselves wasting money and resources in trying to reach new demand. In terms of logistics, hiring more drivers and contracting new fleets may also be wasteful if done without a plan and to ensure maximum efficiency.

Ship from store

With store foot traffic in decline, now is the time for retailers to restructure some stores as MFCs – micro fulfillment centers – effectively 'dark' stores. When operated efficiently, these stores turn into hyperlocal fulfillment centers for multiple fulfillment models, including curbside or click and collect, and in store returns. Turning stores into MFCs is often a pivotal part of guaranteeing same-day fulfillment in urban areas, as service providers can pick up orders and deliver them within hours.

If retailers want to ship from retail stores as well as from distribution centers, they will need to rethink everything from the layout of the staging area, to picking and order prep, and how these steps will impact their store staff's efficiency and performance across other tasks. Logistics providers may have to restructure their operations in order to offer ship-from-store services in urban areas.

Last mile delivery software: A competitive advantage

Manual operations are simply not an option anymore for retailers and logistics providers with large order volumes. Today's innovative tech solutions will allow any company to scale up and optimize their last mile logistics.

Last mile experience – The more innovative brands today use technology to create unique, convenient and automated delivery experiences that help them stay competitive in a saturated market.

Backend flexibility and integrations – good delivery management software will provide the flexibility that dispatchers and operational teams need, including a variety of dispatching models to support varying levels of manual and automated dispatch, based on specific operational requirements and business preferences. All dispatching solutions should include real time visibility across the entire last mile ecosystem, including third party logistics providers.

Last mile solutions that match your business logic – When looking at various software solutions, verify that they will enable you to achieve the necessary efficiencies across your entire ecosystem—from operations to drivers, and finally to end customers—with the core of business focused on the last mile.

Technology makes visibility easy and accurate

Until recently, this stage of the delivery chain was a black hole: Drivers would leave the warehouse or other dispatching center with deliveries on their truck. The status of these deliveries would then remain unknown to both companies and customers until the driver returned to report on it. Today, there are several cloud-based platforms that are changing the status quo for last mile visibility, efficiency and costs.

This includes real time tracking that makes coordination between inventory management systems, warehouses, sorting centers, fulfillment centers, stores and delivery providers easier and smoother.

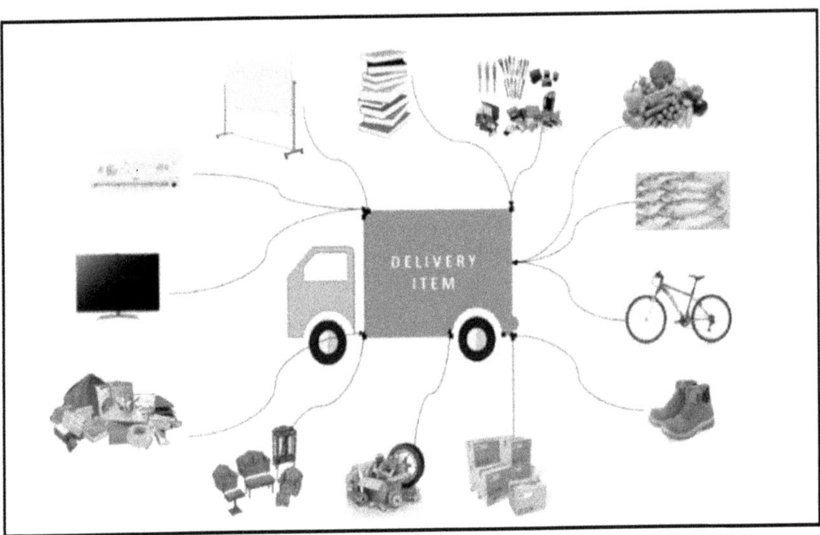

Key factors in last mile success

To orchestrate cost-effective last mile delivery, it is important to identify which delivery models will best serve your business needs – then use delivery and logistics management software to automate, optimize, and scale up your operations.

Operate both on demand and scheduled delivery

Some last mile software can plan both on-demand and scheduled routes, allowing dispatchers to spend their time on other important tasks. Route planning software takes a wide range of factors into account – including parcel size, vehicle size, route, cost of drivers, promised delivery times and more – to create highly efficient, well-planned delivery routes.

These tight timeframes and complex operations require that every component of the last mile delivery process operates in perfect sync. For example, when items are picked from the retail store, every inventory item's location must be precisely mapped, and these retail maps must be updated every time inventory is moved. Manual delivery routing and optimization, particularly for multi-stop deliveries, becomes exceptionally difficult with these tight timelines.

Another important consideration is data collection, quality and synchronization. Operating both on demand and scheduled last mile deliveries require that different teams in an organization operate as a streamlined, efficient assembly line. Everyone from dispatch, to staging teams, to the drivers, shippers and end customers must be kept in the loop with the right information at the right time.

Invest in fleet and driver efficiency

Driver efficiency must remain high to guarantee delivery times and meet customer expectations. Real time updates are crucial for providing visibility for dispatchers and decision-makers, as well as the end customers.

Using automated delivery flow management, drivers can onboard and deliver more easily and intuitively. This system allows additional speed and accuracy and gives drivers the ability to provide updates, collect proof of delivery, signatures, tips and more.

Having access to customized driver management tools allows drivers to accept, create or update orders in real time depending on specific items. Managers have access to tools that allow them to organize based on specific driver, team or fleet as well as tracking locations.

Prioritize the Last Mile Experience

Providing the perfect customer experience depends on efficient, flexible delivery operations – which in turn are based on having the right infrastructure, technology and processes in place.

Last mile delivery software is a key factor in creating an exceptional experience for both brands and consumers, including providing automated notifications for customers from the moment the order is prepared, to when it is en route, to arrival at the final destination.

Send frequent updates and delivery notifications – WIZMI ("where is my order") calls from end customers puts a strain on customer service teams, call centers and other employees. This friction and doubt in the shipping process is one of the first things that should be solved through customer experience technology.

Creating a frictionless delivery process requires technology that enables open communication between the customer and the delivery person, as well as full visibility over their deliveries. Provide customers with updates on order progress at every stage, from the moment it has left the warehouse, distribution center or store, until the moment it arrives.

Customer feedback – Give your customers the opportunity to provide valuable feedback. They will feel satisfied that they can praise you for what you've done well or provide criticism or suggestions to improve on weaker points of your service. Addressing issues affecting customer satisfaction quickly is a major tool in creating brand loyalty.

Multiple delivery options – Brands that give the options of in-store pickup, same day delivery vs. longer but free delivery, delivery with or without assembly, etc. are able to target multiple types of customers at once and satisfy them all.

When it comes to delivery options, it is important to remember that one size doesn't fit all. Some customers prefer to wait a bit longer for their delivery if that means a cheaper option or even a more environmentally friendly option. Others want the option to schedule the day their white glove order arrives. Others will want to order online and pick it up at a local locker or other location at their convenience.

Providing all of these options can be technologically difficult and requires the right tools and systems in place to guarantee that everything arrives on time, when and where the customer expects.

Turning to flexible delivery and fulfillment technology

Flexible technology gives businesses the ability to handle same day and scheduled deliveries under one eCommerce brand. This 'hybrid' model has become increasingly popular in recent years.

Every element of the delivery flow has to be orchestrated so that each stage in the relay will have the optimal amount of time and direction required to meet tight delivery timeframes without affecting quality or reliability. This level of planning and integration of last mile logistics is nearly impossible without technological support.

Technology also allows brands to provide different service plans and levels to different shippers. This flexibility allows brands to expand and contract their last mile delivery capacity, meeting high demand as needed.

The Future of Last Mile Delivery

The eCommerce landscape keeps growing, and logistics will continue to shift in order to accommodate it. To keep up with the market, eCommerce retailers and their logistics partners must adopt best practices and look to solutions that help them provide relevant delivery options and services to their customers, while improving efficiency at every step of the delivery flow. Today's technological tools make maximizing the delivery process easier than ever, allowing brands and last mile logistics providers to maximize efficiency and profits.

While answering their main pain points today, retailers and logistics providers must also ensure they have the tools to manage whatever will be demanded of them in the future. This can be delivering to an alternative fulfillment destination, dispatching autonomous vehicles or a drone, or launching a new fulfillment service.

Frequently asked questions:

What does last mile mean in shipping?

The last mile is the last phase of the delivery process, typically beginning when a customer places an order and ending when the customer receives the package or item. The last mile is critical for online brands, as it highly influences customer satisfaction.

How does last mile delivery work?

The last mile includes 5 steps:
1. Centralized processing for online orders, giving both sides transparency into where the order is.
2. The order goes to the transportation hub
3. Packages go through the process of being assigned or dispatched to specific fleets and then specific routes.
4. Packages leave the transportation hub and are scanned – to make sure that everyone involved is updated on the order status
5. The package makes its way to the final destination

How important is last mile delivery?

Last mile delivery is of the utmost importance to any brand that is selling online. Even while working with external shipping companies, brands must guarantee the best last mile delivery process so that customers receive the best service possible.

T
TranMazon
Amazon Delivery Partner

www.ingramcontent.com/pod-product-compliance
Ingram Content Group UK Ltd.
Pitfield, Milton Keynes, MK11 3LW, UK
UKHW021926190726
13853UKWH00002B/866

9 798416 517014